PROJECT MANAGEMENT

Marion E. Haynes

CRISP PUBLICATIONS, INC.
Los Altos, California

PROJECT MANAGEMENT
Four Steps To Success ·

Marion E. Haynes

CREDITS
Editors: **Michael Crisp and Elaine Fritz**
Designer: **Carol Harris**
Typesetting: **Interface Studio**
Cover Design: **Carol Harris**
Artwork: **Ralph Mapson**

Copyright © 1989 by Crisp Publications, Inc.
Printed in the United States of America

English language Crisp books are distributed worldwide. Our major international distributors include:

CANADA: Reid Publishing Ltd., Box 69559—109 Thomas St., Oakville, Ontario Canada L6J 7R4. TEL: (416) 842-4428, FAX: (416) 842-9327

AUSTRALIA: Career Builders, P. O. Box 1051, Springwood, Brisbane, Queensland, Australia 4127. TEL: 841-1061, FAX: 841-1580

NEW ZEALAND: Career Builders, P. O. Box 571, Manurewa, Auckland, New Zealand. TEL: 266-5276, FAX: 266-4152

JAPAN: Phoenix Associates Co., Mizuho Bldg. 2-12-2, Kami Osaki, Shinagawa-Ku, Tokyo 141, Japan. TEL: 3-443-7231, FAX: 3-443-7640

Selected Crisp titles are also available in other languages. Contact International Rights Manager Tim Polk at (415) 949-4888 for more information.

Library of Congress Catalog Card Number 88-63803
Haynes, Marion E.
Project Management
ISBN 0-931961-75-0

PREFACE

Everyone manages projects from time to time. For example, a student manages a project as part of a class requirement. The do-it-yourselfer manages a project to fix or build something around the house. The host or hostess manages a social affair. These people can capitalize on the same theory of project management that engineers, superintendents, and contractors use. The principles are the same.

Project Management is written to help you carry out your projects successfully. It does not presume any prior knowledge of managerial or technical subjects. The book is divided into six parts to lead you logically through the life of a project. The parts are:

Part 1: Introduction
Part 2: Defining the Project
Part 3: Planning the Project
Part 4: Implementing the Plan
Part 5: Completing the Project
Part 6: Summary

Throughout the book are questionnaires, checklists, and exercises that emphasize the material presented. Work through them as you go along. They will reinforce the concepts you are learning. Successful project management is within your grasp. Simply read, understand, and apply the ideas contained in this book.

Good Luck!

Marion E. Haynes

Marion E. Haynes
Houston, Texas

ABOUT THIS BOOK

Project Management is not like most books. It has a unique, self-paced format that encourages you to become personally involved. Designed to be "read with a pencil," there is an abundance of exercises, activities, checklists, and assessments that invite participation.

The objective of *Project Management* is to help you become a better project manager.

Project Management can be used effectively in a number of ways. Here are some possibilities.

Individual Study. Because the book is self-instructional, all that is needed is a quiet place, some time, and a pencil. By completing the activities and exercises, you not only get valuable feedback, but also practical ideas for self-improvement.

Workshops and Seminars. The book is ideal for assigned reading prior to a workshop or seminar. With the basics already in hand, the quality of participation will improve. More time can then be spent on in-depth understanding of the concept and practical applications during the sessions. The book is also effective when distributed at the beginning of a session; it will provide both structure and content for the training.

Remote Location Training. Copies can be given to those unable to attend centralized training programs.

Informal Study Groups. Thanks to the format, brevity, and low cost, this book is ideal for "brown-bag" or other informal group sessions.

There are other possibilities, depending on the objectives, program, and ideas of the user. One thing is sure: Even after it has been read, this book will serve as excellent reference material that can be easily reviewed.

CONTENTS

PART 1

INTRODUCTION

"WELCOME TO PROJECT MANAGEMENT!"

OBJECTIVES FOR THE READER

When you set objectives, you have a sense of purpose and direction. They define what you are going to accomplish and provide a sense of fulfillment when you achieve them. From the list below, check the objectives that are important to you. Add any specific objectives that improved project management skills will help you achieve.

By completing this book I plan to:

☐ Learn to clarify projects before I start them.

☐ Organize a project so I can complete it within budget and schedule.

☐ Learn to set up a monitoring system that will keep me up-to-date on project status.

☐ Learn to deal with changes to the project plan.

☐ Improve my effectiveness as a project manager.

☐ _____

☐ _____

☐ _____

WHAT IS PROJECT MANAGEMENT?

Project management focuses on a project. A project is an undertaking that has a beginning and an end and is carried out to meet established goals within cost, schedule, and quality objectives. Project management brings together and optimizes the resources necessary to successfully complete the project. These resources include the skills, talents, and cooperative effort of a team of people; facilities, tools, and equipment; information, systems, and techniques; and money.

How Did Project Management Develop?

The concept of project management as a discipline was developed for use in managing the U.S. space program in the early 1960s. Its practice has expanded rapidly into government, the military, and industry. Today you will find these principles being used under the names of *program management, product management,* and *construction management.*

How Does Project Management Differ from Other Management Principles?

Project management differs in two significant ways. **First,** it focuses on a project with a finite life span, whereas departments or other organizational units expect to exist indefinitely. **Second,** projects frequently need resources on a part-time basis, whereas permanent organizations try to utilize resources full-time. The sharing of resources frequently leads to conflict and requires skillful negotiation to see that projects get the necessary resources to meet objectives throughout their project life.

THE PROJECT LIFE CYCLE

Each project moves through a predictable life cycle of four phases with each phase calling for different skills from the project manager. The phases of a project's life cycle are:

- Conceiving and defining the project
- Planning the project
- Implementing the plan
- Completing and evaluating the project

Each phase will be discussed in a chapter of its own later in this book.

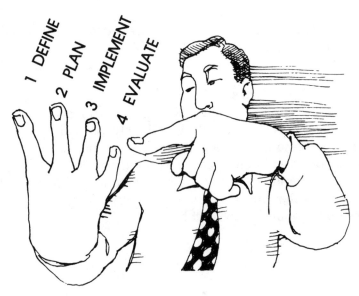

FOUR STEPS TO SUCCESS

Typical Activity Levels During the Phases of a Project's Life

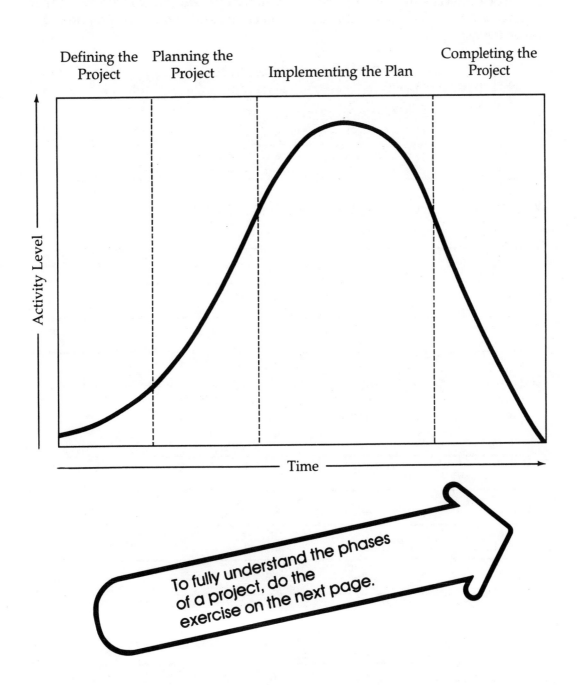

Defining the Project Planning the Project Implementing the Plan Completing the Project

Activity Level

Time

To fully understand the phases of a project, do the exercise on the next page.

6

Exercise

Think of a project you have completed within the last two or three months. It may have been a weekend project at home or something at work. Now, respond to the following questions:

1. When did you first get the idea for the project? How much time elapsed and what steps were involved between the first idea and a clear understanding of what you were going to do?

_____

_____

_____

_____

_____

_____

2. How did you go about planning the project? Did you determine what tools, equipment, and supplies you would need and where to obtain them? Did you plan for extra help if you could not handle the project alone?

_____

_____

_____

_____

_____

_____

3. Once you got under way, did everything go according to plan? Did you stay within budget? Did you finish on time? Did you meet your quality standards? Did any unanticipated problems occur? If so, how did you deal with them?

_____

_____

_____

_____

_____

4. When the project was completed, were there people to be released and reassigned, tools and equipment to be returned, and surplus material to be disposed of?

_____

_____

_____

_____

5. After the project was completed, did you spend any time reflecting on the experience to see where improvements could be made in the management of the project? If not, take a few minutes now and write down some ideas for improvement.

_____

_____

_____

_____

PROJECT PARAMETERS

During a project's life, management focuses on three basic parameters: quality, cost, and time. A successfully managed project is one that is completed at the specified level of quality, on or before the deadline, and within budget.

Each of these parameters is specified in detail during the planning phase of the project. These specifications then form the basis for control during the implementation phase.

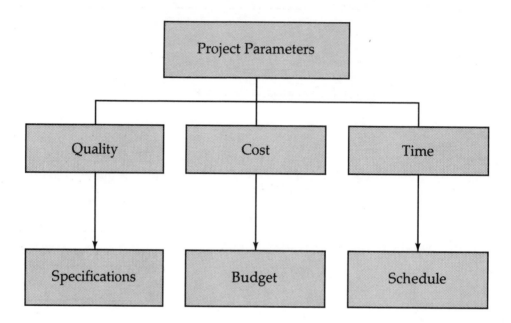

NEGOTIATING SPECIFICATIONS WITH THE CLIENT

If there is a client involved who must accept the project upon completion, the specifications that define a successful outcome must be negotiated and agreed to by the client, and included as part of the contract.

A client may be either internal or external. Also, there may be more than one "client," especially when the project is internal to the company. For example, the case study in this book is a construction project for more space within a company. The clients in this case may be the department that will use the space, and management, who must agree to the budget and scheduling specifications.

In the course of a project, specifications may change. The project manager has responsibility to make sure the client—external or internal—agrees to the revised specifications. If there is a written contract, it needs to be revised and signed off by all involved parties, so that when the final inspection is done, the project team and the client agree on what acceptable parameters are.

Rate Yourself As a Project Manager

Rate yourself on each of the following skills required to be a successful project manager. Place a check mark (✔) in front of each skill you feel you can handle. When you're finished, the ones not checked represent opportunities for development.

My project management skills:

- ☐ Organizing a project from beginning to end.
- ☐ Structuring a plan that will stand up under pressure.
- ☐ Getting people to accept my plans and support them.
- ☐ Setting measurable project objectives.
- ☐ Motivating team members.
- ☐ Helping team members solve problems.
- ☐ Utilizing available resources.
- ☐ Eliminating waste of time and money.
- ☐ Measuring project performance.
- ☐ Using information systems that respond to project needs.

PART 2

DEFINING THE PROJECT

THE ORIGIN OF PROJECTS

Projects grow out of problems or opportunities. At work, they can be initiated by higher management, clients, or staff members. At school, they may be initiated by either teachers, students, or administration; at home, by yourself or other family members. A project is born when someone reacts to the level of frustration surrounding a problem or someone sees an opportunity to move into a new venture. When a decision is made to do something about the problem or opportunity, a project exists—and, typically, someone is given the responsibility of carrying it out. That person becomes the project manager.

What are the Pitfalls, and How Can They Be Avoided?

A project's initiator is almost always unclear about important aspects of the project. Project personnel tend to stress their own points of view during the stage of defining and structuring the project. If this set of personal biases and interests is left unchecked, disaster can result. However, such disaster can be avoided by full discussion between the project manager, client, and staff at the project's inception. With a clear understanding of what is expected, the project manager is now ready to begin defining the project.

GETTING UNDER WAY

GETTING UNDER WAY

When the nucleus of the project team is assembled, its first order of business is to clarify the project and arrive at agreement among team members about the project's definition and scope, as well as the basic strategy for carrying it out. There is an orderly process that can guide you through these steps. The following sequence of activities will get your project smoothly under way:

1. Study, discuss, and analyze.
2. Write the project definition.
3. Set an end-results objective.
4. List imperatives and desirables.
5. Generate alternative strategies.
6. Evaluate alternatives.
7. Choose a course of action.

1. It is critical for the team to spend adequate time at the beginning to *study, discuss, and analyze* the project. This establishes a clear understanding of what you are dealing with. It may be necessary to research how similar projects structured their approach, or what other patterns of past experience can contribute to project planning. The purpose of this activity is to be sure you are addressing the *right* problem or pursuing the *real* opportunity.

2. When you are confident that you have a firm grasp of the situation, work up a *preliminary project definition*. This preliminary definition will be subject to revision as additional information and experience are acquired.

3. Now, using this project definition, state the *end-results objective* of the project.

4. Then, list both the *imperatives and desirables* to be present in the end results. That is, list the outcomes that must be present for the project to be considered successful, and list the outcomes that are not essential but that would add to the project's success.

5. Now you are ready to *generate alternative strategies* that might lead you to your objective. To generate these alternatives, try brainstorming with your project team (see technique on the next page).

6. Next, *evaluate the alternative strategies* you have generated. Be sure that your criteria for evaluation are realistic and reflect the end-results objective.

7. Evaluation allows you to *choose a course of action* that will meet both your project definition and end-results objective.

BRAINSTORMING PROCEDURES FOLLOW

Brainstorming

Brainstorming is a free-form process that taps into the creative potential of a group through association of ideas. Association works as a two-way current: when a group member voices an idea, this stimulates ideas from others, which in turn leads to more ideas from the one who initiated the idea.

Brainstorming Procedures

- ☐ List all ideas offered by group members.

- ☐ Do not evaluate or judge ideas at this time.

- ☐ Do not discuss ideas at this time except to clarify understanding.

- ☐ Welcome ''blue sky'' ideas. It's easier to eliminate ideas later.

- ☐ Repetition is okay. Don't waste time sorting out duplication.

- ☐ Encourage quantity. The more ideas you generate, the greater your chance of finding a useful one.

- ☐ Don't be too anxious to close the process. When a plateau is reached, let things rest and then start again.

TESTING YOUR PRELIMINARY STRATEGY

Before moving to a full-scale project, a feasibility study must be carried out to test your preliminary strategy and answer the basic question: "Will it work?" Depending on the nature of the project, one or more of three alternatives will help answer this question. The choices are to do a *market study, pilot test,* or *computer simulation.*

The amount of money and other resources that are invested in feasibility studies must be in proportion to the amount of money that the project will put at risk. For example, a company that is going to invest $450 million to retool a factory to manufacture a new appliance will probably consider a $250,000 market study an excellent investment if it clarifies the design of the appliance before the major investment is made. On the other hand, a franchised cookie company that is planning to add a new kind of cookie to its line could simply mix up a batch at one store, sell them for a week, and look at sales results—all for a modest investment in local advertising and special ingredients.

Market Study

If your project is to bring a new product to market, you must determine its market potential. Market research asks customers whether your product satisfies their current or potential perceived needs. You can also examine similar products to determine how your product is differentiated from those that are currently available.

Pilot Test

A pilot test is a small-scale tryout of your project. It could be a limited-area market test of a product or a working model of a construction project. Sometimes referred to as "field testing," a pilot test gives you the opportunity to observe your project's performance under actual conditions.

Computer Simulation

Current technology permits many different types of projects to be modeled on computers. For example, the market potential of a product can be predicted by analyzing demographic data of the target users along with certain assumptions about current and potential needs. The load-bearing potential of buildings, bridges, vessels, etc. are analyzed through mathematical calculations.

TESTING YOUR PRELIMINARY STRATEGY (Continued)

Computer simulation is used in such diverse fields as aerodynamics, thermodynamics, optical design, and mechanical design. In some cases, the computer is used to assist with the actual design of the project. The major purpose of simulation is to identify potential problems before the project is built.

Using the Study Results

If the results of a well-conceived and executed feasibility study indicate that the project should proceed, you can move confidently into detailed planning and implementation of your project. If the results are discouraging, the data are used to do a product redesign, followed by another feasibility study, and so on until a successful product concept is identified.

*FEASIBILITY STUDIES SHOULD
BE WELL-CONCEIVED*

PROGRESS REVIEW: PARTS 1 AND 2

Check either *True* or *False* in response to each of the following statements.

True False

1. A project is an ongoing venture or activity.

2. Projects are initiated by whomever is in charge.

3. Anyone can be a project manager.

4. The project manager is responsible for carrying out the project.

5. Quality is not important in projects.

6. The project's initiator usually has a clear idea of all important aspects of the project.

7. Completing a project on time is one important parameter of project management.

8. The project team needs to spend time clearly defining the project before getting under way.

9. Brainstorming has nothing to offer to project management.

10. Completing a project within budget is not important.

11. Your basic strategy for completing a project needs to be tested before moving ahead.

12. A pilot test can be used to evaluate your strategy.

13. Computer simulation can help determine the feasibility of construction projects.

14. Project management is no different than any other application of management principles.

15. The temporary nature of projects leads to unique challenges for project managers.

Score Your Responses

1.—F	4.—T	7.—T	10.—F	13.—T
2.—F	5.—F	8.—T	11.—T	14.—F
3.—T	6.—F	9.—F	12.—T	15.—T

Total Score: _____

12 to 15 *Excellent.* You're ready to move on.
9 to 11 *Good.* A quick review would be helpful before you proceed.
0 to 8 *Poor.* You must have dozed off. Reread Parts 1 and 2.

PART 3

PLANNING THE PROJECT

PLANNING THE THREE PROJECT PARAMETERS

Planning is crucial in project management. Planning means listing in detail what is required to successfully complete the project along the three critical dimensions of quality, time, and cost. Each of these dimensions will be considered in the following pages, along with a variety of tools and techniques.

Planning Steps

☐ Establish the project objective.

☐ Choose a basic strategy for achieving the objective.

☐ Break the project down into subunits or steps.

☐ Determine the performance standards for each subunit.

☐ Determine how much time is required to complete each subunit.

☐ Determine the proper sequence for completing the subunits and aggregate this information into a schedule for the total project.

☐ Design the cost of each subunit and aggregate costs into the project budget.

☐ Design the necessary staff organization, including the number and kind of positions, and the duties and responsibilities of each.

☐ Determine what training, if any, is required for project team members.

☐ Develop the necessary policies and procedures.

PLANNING THE QUALITY DIMENSION

Planning for quality* requires attention to detail. The goal of quality planning is to assure that the output of the project will perform—that it will do what it is supposed to do. The quality plan also establishes the criteria of performance by which the project output will be measured when it is completed.

In planning the quality dimension, include specifications for the quality and types of materials to be used, the performance standards to be met, and the means of verifying quality such as testing and inspection. Two techniques facilitate planning for quality: a *work breakdown structure* and *project specifications*. Both are described on the next few pages.

PROJECT QUALITY IS DEFINED BY
DETAILED PROJECT SPECIFICATIONS

---

*For an excellent book on this topic, order *Quality at Work* from the back of this book.

Creating a Work Breakdown Structure

A work breakdown structure is the starting place for planning all three parameters of a project: quality, cost, and time. It's a technique based on dividing a project into subunits or work packages. Because all elements required to complete the project are identified, you reduce the chances of neglecting or overlooking an essential step.

A work breakdown structure is typically constructed with two or three levels of detail, although more levels may be required for very complex projects. Start by identifying logical subdivisions of the project, then break each of these down further. As you construct a work breakdown structure, keep in mind that the goal is to identify a unit of work that is discrete and that advances the project toward its completion.

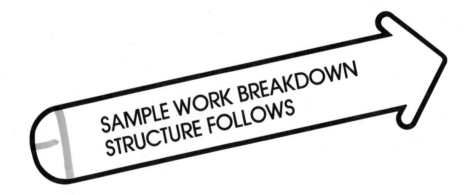

SAMPLE WORK BREAKDOWN STRUCTURE FOLLOWS

CASE STUDY: REMODELING PROJECT

Sample Work Breakdown Structure

Project Definition: Remodel Building #7 to provide four additional offices by the end of the third quarter at a cost not to exceed $17,500.

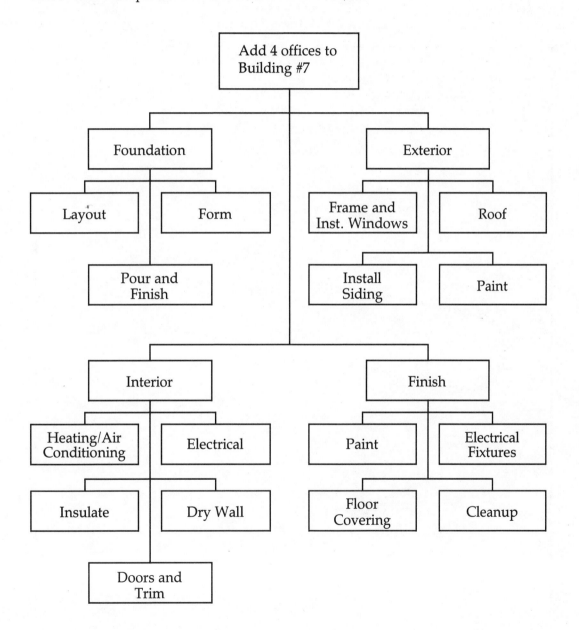

Practice Making a Work Breakdown Structure

Select a project you have completed or plan to complete and break it down into subunits (components or steps). Draw a work breakdown structure showing the relationship among the subunits.

Work Breakdown Structure

Project Specifications

From the work breakdown structure, specifications can be written for each subunit of the project. Specifications include all relevant requirements to meet the project's quality dimension—materials to be used, standards to be met, tests to be performed, etc. Use extreme care in writing specifications, because they become the controlling factor in meeting project performance standards, and directly affect both budget and schedule.

Example of Project Specifications

Foundation

- Pour 4-inch concrete slab over 6 inches of compacted sand fill. Reinforce with 6-inch by 6-inch #6 wire mash. Install 6 mil polyethylene membrane water-proofing barrier between sand and concrete.

- Use 1-foot wide by 1-foot 6-inch deep beams around perimeter of foundation and under loadbearing walls, per blueprints. Beams to include #5 reinforcing steel bars in each corner positioned with #3 stirrups on 2-feet 6-inch centers.

- Concrete to withstand 2500 psi test after 28 days.

Practice Writing Project Specifications

Take the project for which you made a work breakdown structure and write specifications for at least one subunit of the project.

_____

_____

_____

_____

_____

_____

_____

_____

_____

_____

PLANNING THE TIME DIMENSION

The objective when planning the time dimension is to determine the shortest time necessary to complete the project. Begin with the work breakdown structure and determine the time required to complete each subunit. Next, determine in what sequence subunits must be completed, and which ones may be under way at the same time. From this analysis, you will have determined the three most significant time elements:

> - The duration of each step
>
> - The earliest time at which a step may be started
>
> - The latest time at which a step must be started

Planning the time dimension can only be done by people who have experience with the same or similar activities. If you personally do not know how long it takes to do something, you will need to rely on someone else who does have the requisite experience.

Many project managers find it realistic to estimate time intervals as a range rather than as a precise amount. Another way to deal with the lack of precision in estimating time is to use a commonly accepted formula for that task. Or, if you are working with a mathematical model, you can determine the probability of the work being completed within the estimated time by calculating a standard deviation of the time estimate.

Using a Mathematical Model to Estimate Time

Estimating Time

Tm—The most probable time

To —The optimistic (shortest) time within which only 1% of similar projects are completed

Tp —The pessimistic (longest) time within which 99% of similar projects are completed

Te —The calculated time estimate

$$Te = \frac{To + 4\,Tm + Tp}{6}$$

σ = Standard deviation

$$\sigma = \frac{Tp - To}{6}$$

- 68.26% of the time the work will be completed within the range of *Te* ± 1 standard deviation.

- 95.44% of the time the work will be completed within the range of *Te* ± 2 standard deviations.

- 99.73% of the time the work will be completed within the range of *Te* ± standard deviations.

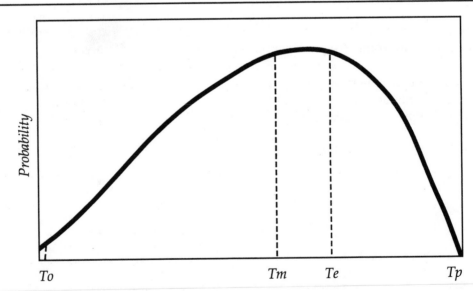

With a time duration determined for each subunit of the project, the next step is to determine the earliest and latest starting times for each subunit. There are two commonly used methods for charting the project: Gantt charts and PERT diagrams. The details of these two methods are discussed on the following pages.

Practice Estimating Time

Using the same project, determine a time estimate for each of the project's subunits or steps.

Subunit or Step	To	Tp	Tm	Te

Gantt Charts

A Gantt chart is a horizontal bar chart that graphically displays the time relationship of the steps in a project. It is named after Henry Gantt, the industrial engineer who introduced the procedure in the early 1900s. Each step of a project is represented by a line placed on the chart in the time period when it is to be undertaken. When completed, the Gantt chart shows the flow of activities in sequence as well as those that can be under way at the same time.

To create a Gantt chart, list the steps required to complete a project and estimate the time required for each step. Then list the steps down the left side of the chart and time intervals along the bottom. Draw a line across the chart for each step, starting at the planned beginning date and ending on the completion date of that step.

Some parallel steps can be carried out at the same time with one taking longer than the other; this allows some flexibility about when to start the shorter step, as long as the plan has it finished in time to flow into subsequent steps. This situation can be shown with a dotted line continuing on to the time when the step must be completed.

When your Gantt chart is finished, you will be able to see the minimum total time for the project, the proper sequence of steps, and which steps can be under way at the same time.

Example of a Gantt Chart

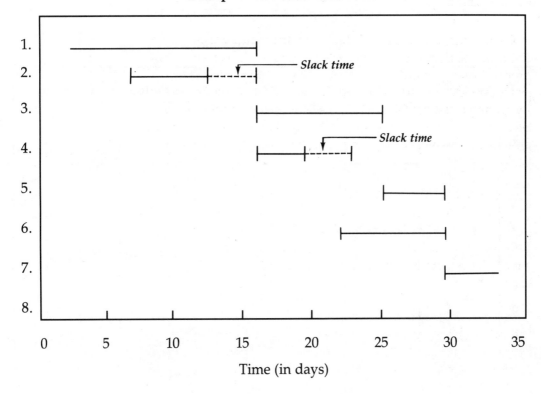

You can add to the usefulness of a Gantt chart by also charting actual progress. This is usually done by drawing a line in a different color below the original line to show the actual beginning and ending dates of each step. This allows you to quickly assess whether or not the project is on schedule.

Gantt charts are limited in their ability to show the interdependencies of activities. In projects where the steps flow in a simple sequence of events, they can portray adequate information for project management. However, when several steps are under way at the same time and a high level of interdependency exists among the various steps, PERT diagrams are a better choice.

CASE STUDY: REMODELING PROJECT

Example of a Gantt Chart

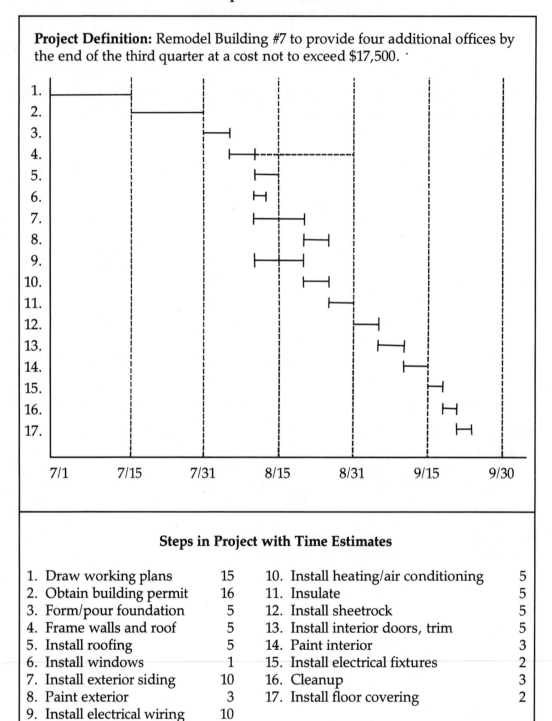

Project Definition: Remodel Building #7 to provide four additional offices by the end of the third quarter at a cost not to exceed $17,500. ·

Steps in Project with Time Estimates

1. Draw working plans	15	
2. Obtain building permit	16	
3. Form/pour foundation	5	
4. Frame walls and roof	5	
5. Install roofing	5	
6. Install windows	1	
7. Install exterior siding	10	
8. Paint exterior	3	
9. Install electrical wiring	10	

10. Install heating/air conditioning	5	
11. Insulate	5	
12. Install sheetrock	5	
13. Install interior doors, trim	5	
14. Paint interior	3	
15. Install electrical fixtures	2	
16. Cleanup	3	
17. Install floor covering	2	

Practice Drawing a Gantt Chart

Using the project you prepared a work breakdown structure for earlier, estimate the time required for each step. Then draw a Gantt chart for the project.

Project: _____

_____

_____

Project Steps with Time Estimates

(in _____)

STEP	TIME	STEP	TIME
_____	____	_____	____
_____	____	_____	____
_____	____	_____	____
_____	____	_____	____
_____	____	_____	____
_____	____	_____	____
_____	____	_____	____
_____	____	_____	____
_____	____	_____	____
_____	____	_____	____

Gantt Chart

PERT Diagrams

PERT stands for Program Evaluation and Review Technique. It is a more sophisticated form of planning than Gantt charts, and is appropriate for projects with many interactive steps. There are three components of a PERT diagram: *Events* are represented by circles or other convenient, closed figures; *activities* are represented by arrows connecting the circles; and *non-activities* connecting two events are shown as dotted-line arrows. (A non-activity represents a dependency between two events for which no work is required.)

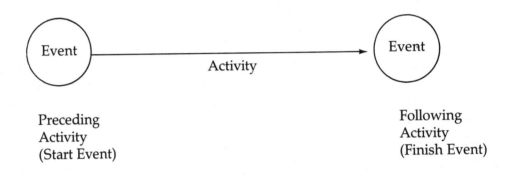

PERT diagrams are most useful if they show the time scheduled for completing an activity on the activity line. Time is recorded in a unit appropriate for the project, with days being most common, and hours, weeks, or even months occasionally used. Some diagrams show two numbers for time estimates—a high estimate and a low estimate.

The most sophisticated PERT diagrams are drawn on a time scale, with the horizontal projection of connecting arrows drawn to represent the amount of time required for their activity. In the process of diagraming to scale, some connecting arrows will be longer than completion of that task requires. This represents slack time in the project and is depicted by a heavy dot at the end of the appropriate time period, followed by a dotted-line arrow connecting with the following event.

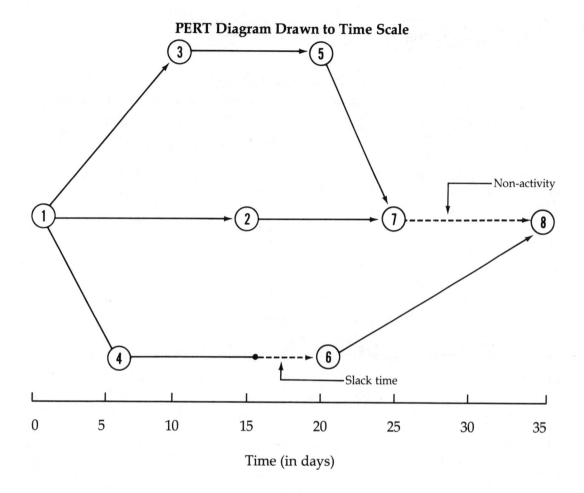

PERT Diagram Drawn to Time Scale

Time (in days)

To draw a PERT diagram, list the steps required to finish a project and estimate the time required to complete each step. Then draw a network of relationships among the steps, keeping in mind the importance of proper sequencing. The number of the step from your list is written in the appropriate event circle to identify that step. The time to complete the following step is shown on the arrow. Steps that can be under way at the same time are shown on different paths. Be sure to include all the elements shown on your work breakdown structure.

A PERT diagram not only shows the relationship among various steps in a project, but also serves as an easy way to calculate the *critical path*. The critical path is the longest path through the network and as such identifies essential steps that must be completed on time to avoid delay in completing the project. The critical path is shown as a heavy line in the following example.

The usefulness of a PERT diagram can be increased by coloring each step as it is completed. Actual time can be written over the estimated time to maintain a running tally of actual versus planned time along the critical path.

CASE STUDY: REMODELING PROJECT

PERT Diagram

Project Definition: Remodel Building #7 to provide four additional offices by the end of the third quarter at a cost not to exceed $17,500.

Note: Numbers in the circles correspond to the steps listed below. Numbers on the lines show the days required to complete the following step.

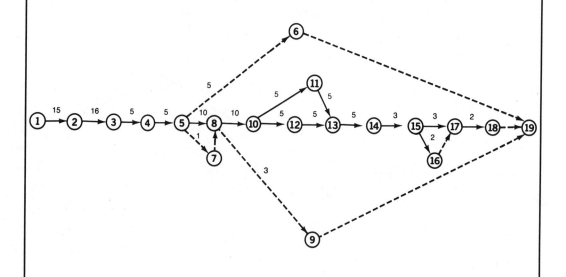

Steps in Project with Time Estimates
(in days)

1. Project started	—	11. Heating/air conditioning in	5
2. Working plans completed	15	12. Insulation	5
3. Building permit obtained	16	13. Sheetrock hung	5
4. Foundation poured	5	14. Interior doors/trim installed	5
5. Walls/roof framed	5	15. Interior painted	3
6. Roofing completed	5	16. Electrical fixtures installed	2
7. Windows installed	1	17. Cleanup completed	3
8. Exterior siding installed	10	18. Floor covering installed	2
9. Exterior painted	3	19. Project completed	—
10. Electrical wiring in	10		

Practice Drawing a PERT Diagram

Select a project, break it down into steps, estimate the time required to complete each step, and draw a PERT diagram for the project.

Project: _____

_____

_____

Project Steps with Time Estimates

STEP	TIME	STEP	TIME
_____	___	_____	___
_____	___	_____	___
_____	___	_____	___
_____	___	_____	___
_____	___	_____	___
_____	___	_____	___
_____	___	_____	___
_____	___	_____	___
_____	___	_____	___
_____	___	_____	___

PERT Diagram

PLANNING THE COST DIMENSION

There are many reasons to do careful planning for project costs. To begin with, if you overestimate costs you may lose the job before you begin because you are not competitive. A good plan includes the identification of sources of supplies and materials, and this careful research assures that the costs are realistic. The main function of a good budget is to monitor the costs of a project while it is in progress, and to avoid cost overruns.

Some inaccuracies in the budget are inevitable, but they should not be the consequence of insufficient work on the original plan. The goal is to be as realistic as possible.

You cannot estimate the cost of your project until you know how long it will take, since the time of labor is typically the most significant cost item. Therefore, use your work breakdown structure and project schedule as the starting point for developing your project budget.

Typical Costs Components

- Labor

- Overhead

- Materials

- Supplies

- Equipment rental

- General and administrative

- Profit (if applicable)

Cost Components Defined

- *Labor:* The wages paid to all staff directly working on the project for the time spent on it.

- *Overhead:* The cost of payroll taxes and fringe benefits for everyone directly working on the project for the time spent on it. Usually calculated as a percentage of direct labor cost.

- *Materials:* The cost of items purchased for use in the project. Includes such things as lumber, cement, steel, nails, screws, rivets, bolts, and paint.

- *Supplies:* The cost of tools, equipment, office supplies, etc., needed for the project. If something has a useful life beyond the project, its cost should be prorated.

- *Equipment rental:* The cost of renting equipment such as scaffolding, compressors, cranes, bulldozers, trucks, etc., for use on the project.

- *General and Administrative:* The cost of management and support services such as purchasing, accounting, secretarial, etc., for time dedicated to the project. Usually calculated as a percentage of project cost.

- *Profit:* In a for-profit project, the reward to the firm for successfully completing the project. Usually calculated as a percentage of project cost.

With the cost components identified and the project broken down into subunits, create a worksheet to tally the costs for the total project.

Note that costing a subunit is sometimes simplified if it is to be subcontracted. Costing then includes bidding the subunit, selecting a contractor, and then using the contract price as your cost.

CASE STUDY: CONSTRUCTION PROJECT

Project Costing Worksheet
(Prepared by General Contractor)

SUBUNIT (COMPONENT OR STEP)	LABOR	OVER-HEAD	MATERIALS	SUPPLIES	EQUIPMENT RENTAL	GEN & ADMIN.	PROFIT	TOTAL
1. Complete working plans	300	75		50		25	50	500
2. Obtain building permit						50		50
3. Pour foundation	500	125	1,300	100	100	125	250	2,500
4. Frame/install windows	500	125	1,500	75	300	150	300	2,950
5. Install roofing	400	100	500		75	50	125	1,250
6. Install exterior siding	700	175	1,800	100	500	150	375	3,800
7. Paint exterior	160	40	25		50		25	300
8. Heating/air conditioning	300	75	1,175			75	175	1,800
9. Electrical wiring	300	75	175			25	75	650
10. Insulation	300	75	300				75	750
11. Hang dry wall	400	100	300			25	75	900
12. Install doors, trim	200	50	350		50	25	25	700
13. Paint interior	200	50	25				75	350
14. Install electrical fixtures	50		100					150
15. Install floor covering	100	25	200			25	50	400
16. Cleanup	100	25		25				150
Total	4,510	1,115	7,750	350	1,075	725	1,675	17,200

Practice Costing a Project

Prepare a cost estimate for the project you have been using. Use as many of the cost columns as apply.

SUBUNIT (COMPONENT OR STEP)								
TOTAL								

ASSIGNING RESPONSIBILITY

Determining who will have responsibility for completing each subunit or step of a project should be done as early as possible, so that they can participate in the planning of both schedules and budgets. This participation leads to a greater commitment to achieve the project within time and cost limitations.

The number of people involved in a project varies with its size and scope. Not every project has a different person responsible for each subunit.

To make the best use of your resources when deciding who is responsible for a portion of your project, broaden your point of view to include subcontractors and service departments as well as members of the project team.

DON'T BE AFRAID OF RESPONSIBILITY

Practice Making a Planning Summary Worksheet

Select a project, break it down into its components or steps, estimate the time required and cost for each subunit, and identify the person or group responsible for carrying it out.

Project: _____

_____

_____

COMPONENT OR STEP	BUDGET	SCHEDULE	RESPONSIBILITY

PROGRESS REVIEW: PART 3

Check either *True* or *False* in response to each of the following statements.

True   False

☐   ☐   1. Planning is not necessary on small projects.

☐   ☐   2. A work breakdown structure is the starting point for planning a project.

☐   ☐   3. Job specifications detail the requirements for project quality.

☐   ☐   4. Tests should be a part of specifications.

☐   ☐   5. When developing a project schedule, the duration and sequence of each step is important.

☐   ☐   6. The latest time a step can begin is not significant in the planning process.

☐   ☐   7. Experience is the only basis for estimating time requirements.

☐   ☐   8. A Gantt chart graphically displays the time relationship of each step in a project.

☐   ☐   9. A Gantt chart clearly displays the interdependencies of project steps.

☐   ☐   10. A PERT diagram is more sophisticated than a Gantt chart.

☐   ☐   11. The critical path is the shortest total time through a PERT diagram.

True   False

☐   ☐   12. In cost planning, overhead includes general and administrative expenses.

☐   ☐   13. Those responsible for subunits of a project should not be included in planning.

☐   ☐   14. Training project personnel is the responsibility of the Human Resources Department, and therefore should not be of any concern to the project manager.

☐   ☐   15. Establishing project policies and responsibilities is a part of project planning.

Score Your Responses

1.—F	4.—T	7.—T	10.—T	13.—F
2.—T	5.—T	8.—T	11.—F	14.—F
3.—T	6.—F	9.—F	12.—F	15.—T

Total Score: ———

12 to 15   *Excellent.* You understand project planning. Proceed to the next topic.

9 to 11   *Good.* Look back over the material to pick up what you missed the first time.

0 to 8   *Poor.* Take a break and then reread Part 3. This time be sure to complete the exercises.

PART 4

IMPLEMENTING THE PLAN

WHAT HAPPENS IN THE IMPLEMENTATION STAGE

During the implementation phase, the project manager coordinates all the elements of a project. This involves a number of responsibilities: controlling work in progress to see that it is carried out according to plan; providing feedback to those working on the project; negotiating for materials, supplies, and services; and resolving differences among those involved with the project. These responsibilities require a variety of skills. This section presents tools and techniques to help project managers during the implementation stage.

Key Duties During Implementation

- Controlling work in progress

- Providing feedback

- Negotiating for materials, supplies, and services

- Resolving differences

CONTROLLING WORK IN PROGRESS

Controlling is the central activity during implementation. The most important tool in this process is the plan that was developed to define the three parameters of the project—specifications, schedule, and budget. These are the standards against which performance is measured. Controlling involves three steps:

> 1. Establishing standards
>
> 2. Monitoring performance
>
> 3. Taking corrective action

1. Establishing Standards

Standards for the project were set in the detailed project specifications created in the planning stage. The project manager must constantly refer to these specifications and make sure the project team is also referencing them. If the project deviates from the original specifications, there is no guarantee that the success predicted by the feasibility studies will actually happen—the product or project outcome might fail to meet performance standards.

There are a number of tools available to help project managers control the project and make sure that the parameters defined in the specifications for quality, time, and budget are actually being met. A Gantt chart or PERT diagram designed at the planning stage is a great device for tracking how the time dimesion of the project is proceeding in relationship to plan.

In the following pages we will describe four additional charts that are useful for project control:

- Control point identification charts

- Project control charts

- Milestone charts

- Budget control charts

Control Point Identification Charts

A helpful technique for controlling a project is to invest some time to think through what is likely to go wrong in each of the three project parameters. Then identify when and how you will know that something is amiss and what you will do to correct the problem if it occurs. This will help minimize the times you will be caught by surprise as well as save time in responding to the problem. A control point identification chart is an easy way to summarize this information:

Example Control Point Identification Chart

CONTROL ELEMENT	WHAT IS LIKELY TO GO WRONG?	HOW AND WHEN WILL I KNOW?	WHAT WILL I DO ABOUT IT?
Quality	Workmenship of craftsman might be less than desired.	Upon personal inspection of each stage of project.	Have sub-standard work redone.
Cost	Cost of any subunit of Project may exceed budget.	When purchase agreements are made.	First, seek alternative suppliers, then, consider alternative materials.
Timeliness	Time to complete any subunit of project may exceed schedule.	By closely monitoring actual progress against schedule along critical path.	Look for ways to improve efficiency, attempt to capture time from later steps, authorize overtime if budget permits.

Practicing Making a Control Point Identification Chart

Select a project and think through each of the questions relating to the three project parameters.

Project: _____

_____

_____

CONTROL ELEMENT	WHAT IS LIKELY TO GO WRONG?	HOW AND WHEN WILL I KNOW?	WHAT WILL I DO ABOUT IT?
Quality			
Cost			
Timeliness			

Project Control Charts

Another helpful tool is a project control chart, which uses budget and schedule plans in a quick status report of the project. It compares actual to planned, calculates a variance on each subunit completed, and tallies a cumulative variance for the project.

To prepare a project control chart, refer to the work breakdown structure and list all of the subunits of the project. Then, use the schedule to list the time planned to complete each subunit, and use the budget to list the expected cost of each subunit.

As each project subunit is completed, record the actual time and actual cost. Calculate variances and carry the cumulative total forward.

This technique can easily be put into a spreadsheet format on your personal computer. Some large projects may be able to create this format for a report that uses cost and schedule data that is routinely captured by the company's computerized accounting system.

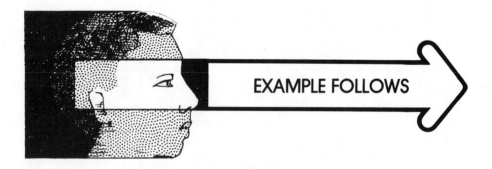

EXAMPLE FOLLOWS

CASE STUDY: CONSTRUCTION PROJECT

Project Costing Chart

Project: Remodel Building #7 to provide four additional offices by the end of the 3rd quarter at a cost not to exceed $17,500.

	COST				SCHEDULE			
PROJECT STEPS	BUDGET	ACTUAL	VARIANCE	TOTAL	PLANNED	ACTUAL	VARIANCE	TOTAL
1. Draw working plans	500	450	(50)	(50)	15	15	—	0
2. Obtain building permit	50	50	—	(50)	16	15	(1)	(1)
3. Form/pour foundation	2,500	2,750	250	200	5	3	(2)	(3)
4. Frame walls/roof	2,200	2,100	(100)	100	5	5	—	(3)
5. Install roofing	1,250	1,500	250	350	5*	6	1	(3)
6. Install windows	750	750	—	350	1*	1	—	(3)
7. Install exterior siding	3,800	3,350	(450)	(100)	10	9	(1)	(4)
8. Paint exterior	300				3			
9. Intall electrical wiring	650				10*			
10. Install heating & A/C	1,800				5			
11. Insulate	750				5			
12. Install sheetrock	900				5			
13. Install doors/trim	700				5			
14. Paint interior	350				3			
15. Install electrical fixtures	150				2			
16. Cleanup	150				3			
17. Install floor covering	400				2			
18. Project completion (Total)	17,400				84			

*Not on critical path—excluded from total.

The project control chart on the following page may be reproduced for your own use.

Project Control Chart

PROJECT STEPS	COST				SCHEDULE			
	BUDGET	ACTUAL	VARIANCE	TOTAL	PLANNED	ACTUAL	VARIANCE	TOTAL

Milestone Charts

A milestone chart presents a broad-brush picture of a project's schedule and control dates. It lists those key events that are clearly verifiable by others or that require approval before the project can proceed. If this is done correctly, a project will not have many milestones. Because of this lack of detail, a milestone chart is not very helpful during the planning phase when more information is required. However, it is particularly useful in the implementation phase because it provides a concise summary of the progress of the project.

Example of Milestone Chart

MILESTONE	SCHEDULED COMPLETION	ACTUAL COMPLETION
1. Foundation completed	August 5	August 2
2. Framing completed	August 10	August 7
3. Exterior finished	August 25	
4. Electrical wiring completed	August 20	
5. Heating and air conditioning installed	August 25	
6. Interior finished	September 22	

Budget Control Charts

Budget control charts are generally of two varieties. One is a listing of the subunits of a project with actual costs compared to budget. They are similar to project control charts, discussed earlier, and can be either hand- or computer-generated. The other kind is a graph of budgeted costs compared to actual. Either bar or line graphs may be used. Bar graphs usually relate budgeted and actual costs by project subunits, while line graphs usually relate planned cumulative project costs to actual costs over time.

Example of a Budget Control Chart

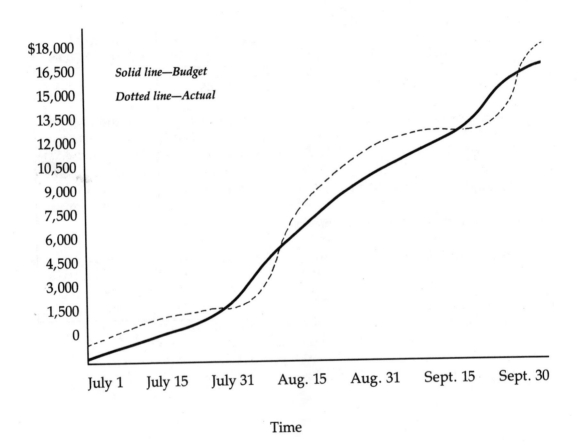

Solid line—Budget

Dotted line—Actual

Time

2. Monitoring Performance

The heart of the control process is monitoring work in progress. It is your way of knowing what is going on—how actual compares to plan. With effective monitoring, you will know if and when corrective action is required. Common ways to keep abreast of project progress are:

- Inspection

- Interim progress reviews

- Testing

- Auditing

Inspection is probably the most common way to monitor project performance. It is handled by trained inspectors as well as by the project manager. Get out into the area where the work is performed and observe what is going on. Inspection is an effective way to see whether project specifications are being met, as well as whether there is unnecessary waste or unsafe work practices. Inspections should be unannounced and on a random schedule. However, they should also be open and direct. Ask questions and listen to explanations.

Interim progress reviews are communications between the project manager and those responsible for the various subunits of a project. Progress reviews can be in a group or on an individual basis, and either face-to-face or by telephone. Alternatively, progress reports can be submitted in writing. Progress reviews typically occur on a fixed time schedule—daily or weekly, or keyed to the completion of project subunits. These scheduled reviews are typically augumented by reviews called by either the project manager or the one responsible for the work. (Guidelines for conducting progress reviews follow.)

Monitoring Performance (Continued)

Testing is another way to verify project quality. Certain tests are usually written into the specifications to confirm that the desired quality is being achieved. Typical tests include pressure or stress tests on mechanical components.

Auditing can be done during the course of a project as well as at its conclusion. Common areas for audit are financial recordkeeping, purchasing practices, safety practices, security practices, maintenance procedures, and authority for disbursement. Auditors should be experts in the area of the project under review, and are typically not members of the project team. After carefully examining the area under review, a report is written describing in detail what was found and pointing out practices that deviate from established policy, authorized procedures, or sound business practices.

Effective monitoring includes more than one source of information. In addition to data from either hand- or computer-generated records, a combination of inspections, progress reviews, testing, and auditing will round out your information and keep you up-to-date on the status of your project.

AUDITS CAN BE EFFECTIVE

Conducting Interim Progress Reviews

Interim progress reviews typically occur on a fixed time schedule, such as daily or weekly. They may also occur when some problem in performance is observed or at the completion of a significant step toward the accomplishment of the project. Three topics are usually on the agenda:

- Review of progress against plan

- Review of problems encountered and how they were handled

- Review of anticipated problems with proposed plans for handling them

---

Your role during an interim progress review is to achieve your objectives of knowing the status of operations and influence the course of future events as necessary. During the discussion, you may have any of the following roles:

Listener: Listen as the individual updates you on progress, deviation from plan, problems encountered, and solutions proposed. Listen not only to what is said, but also to *how* things are said. Is the person excited, frustrated, discouraged? Help clarify what is being said by asking questions, and verify what you think is being said by restating your understanding of both facts and feelings.

Conducting Interim Progress Reviews (Continued)

Contributor: In many interim reviews, progress is in line with plans. However, you will occasionally have problems to deal with. When this occurs, you can contribute to their solution by directing the other person toward possible courses of action. Use your knowledge and experience as necessary to move the project forward.

Integrator: An important role of project managers is to integrate the individual parts of a project into a compatible whole. Is something being neglected? Is there duplication of effort? How can the people available be best deployed?

Leader: Perhaps the most important role for the project manager is that of leader. Through a variety of techniques, you must keep the team's effort directed toward the common goal of completing the project according to specifications, on time, and within budget. You must confirm and recognize good performance, correct poor performance, and keep interest and enthusiasm high.

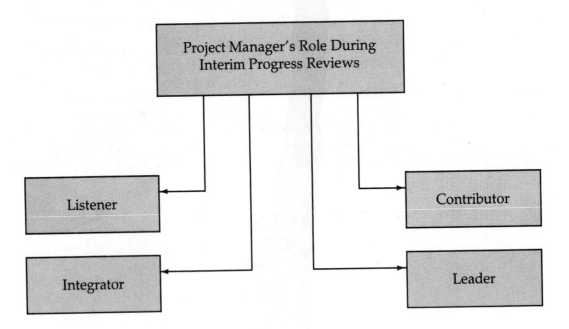

3. Taking Corrective Action

As a project progresses and you monitor performance, there will be times when actual does not measure up to plan. This calls for corrective action. However, don't be too quick to take action. Some deficiencies turn out to be self-correcting. It is unrealistic to expect steady and consistent progress day after day. Sometimes you'll fall behind and sometimes you'll be ahead, but in a well-planned project, you will probably finish on schedule and within budget.

When quality is not according to specification, the customary action is to do it over according to plan. However, this needs to be more closely examined in some instances. For example, if the work or material exceeds specifications, you may choose to accept it. If it falls short, you need to consider how much it deviates from specifications and whether the deficiency will cause the project to fail its performance evaluation. The final decision may be to have the work redone, but that is not an automatic outcome.

When the project begins to fall behind in schedule, there are three alternatives that may correct the problem. The first is to examine the work remaining to be done and decide whether the lost time can be recovered in the next steps. If this is not feasible, consider offering an incentive for on-time completion of the project. The incentive could be justified if you compare this expenditure to potential losses due to late completion. Finally, consider deploying more resources. This too will cost more, but may offset further losses from delayed completion.

When the project begins to exceed budget, consider the work remaining and whether or not cost overruns can be recouped on work yet to be completed. If this isn't practical, consider narrowing the project scope or obtaining more funding from your client.

What to Do When You Start Falling Behind

ACTION	COST	SCHEDULE
1. **Renegotiate:** Discuss with your client the prospect of increasing the budget for the project or extending the deadline for completion.	X	X
2. **Recover During Later Steps:** If you begin to fall behind in early steps of a project, reexamine budgets and schedules for later steps. Perhaps you can save on later steps so the overall budget and/or schedule is met.	X	X
3. **Narrow Project Scope:** Perhaps nonessential elements of the project can be eliminated, thereby reducing costs and/or saving time.	X	X
4. **Deploy More Resources:** You may need to put more people or machines on the project to meet a critical schedule. Increased costs must be weighed against the importance of the deadline.		X
5. **Accept Substitution:** When something is not available or is more expensive than budgeted, substituting a comparable item may solve your problem.	X	X
6. **Seek Alternative Sources:** When a supplier can't deliver within budget or schedule, look for others who can. (You may choose to accept a substitute rather than seek other sources.)	X	X
7. **Accept Partial Delivery:** Sometimes a supplier can deliver a partial order to keep your project on schedule and complete the delivery later.		X
8. **Offer Incentives:** Go beyond the scope of the original contract and offer a bonus or other incentive for on-time delivery.		X
9. **Demand Compliance:** Sometimes demanding that people do what they agreed to do gets the desired results. You may have to appeal to higher management for backing and support.	X	X

PROVIDING FEEDBACK

Project managers find many opportunities to provide feedback to those who have a hand in completing the project. Through feedback, individuals learn about the effect their behavior has on others and on the project's success. It serves to maintain good performance and correct poor performance. To be effective, however, feedback must be handled properly. This illustration shows the continuous loop that exists when there is good feedback:

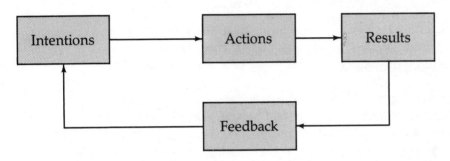

The most important guideline when providing feedback is to deal only with what you can observe. This limits your conversation to actions and results, because you cannot observe someone's intentions.

When offering positive feedback, describe the actions and results in a straightforward way and include an appropriate statement of your reaction. For example, you might tell someone, ''By staying late last night and finishing the work you were doing, the project was able to move forward on schedule. I appreciate your putting out the extra effort.''

Negative feedback can be handled in the same manner, but an important element is missing: how the team member should deal with similar situations in the future. The following sequence should prove more effective:

Handling Negative Feedback

1. Describe the observed actions and results.

2. Ask the individual if those were his or her intended results.

3. With a typical ''No'' response, ask what different actions would likely produce the desired results.

4. Discuss different alternative courses of action.

5. Agree upon a way to handle similar situations if they should occur in the future.

Check Your Feedback Style

Rate yourself by placing a check mark (✓) in front of each action that is typical of how you handle giving feedback. The ones you don't check represent opportunities for development.

☐ *Describe rather than evaluate.* By describing observed action and results, the individual is free to use or not use the information. By avoiding evaluation, you reduce the likelihood of a defensive reaction.

☐ *Be specific rather than general.* Avoid using "always" and "never." Rather, discuss specific times and events. Avoid generalized conclusions such as "you're too dominating." Rather, be specific by saying, "When you don't listen to others, you may miss a valuable idea."

☐ *Deal with behavior that can be changed.* Frustration is increased when you remind someone of a shortcoming over which he or she has no control.

☐ *Be timely.* Generally, feedback is most useful at the earliest opportunity after the behavior.

☐ *Communicate clearly.* This is particularly important when handling negative feedback. One way to ensure clear communication is to have the receiver rephrase the feedback to see if it corresponds to what you had in mind.

OBTAINING QUALITY FEEDBACK

NEGOTIATING FOR MATERIALS, SUPPLIES, AND SERVICES

Negotiating* is an important process that takes up as much as 20% of a manager's time. Negotiating is one way to resolve differences, and it can contribute significantly to the success of your project.

The ideas presented here will prepare you to negotiate effectively.

Definition

Negotiation is a discussion between two parties with a goal of reaching agreement on issues that separate them when neither party has the power (or the desire to use its power) to force an outcome.

THEY NEED TO LEARN HOW TO NEGOTIATE

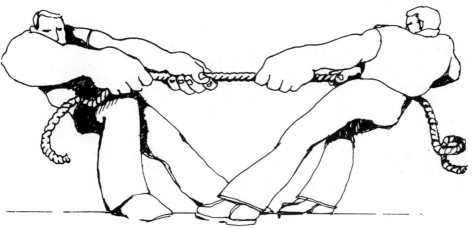

---

*For an excellent book on this topic, order *Successful Negotiation* from the back of this book.

Ten Guidelines for Effective Negotiation

1. **Prepare:** Do your homework. Know what outcome you want and why. Find out what outcome the other party wants. Avoid negotiating when you are not prepared—ask for the time you need. As part of your preparation, figure out what you will do if you are unable to come to an agreement. Your power in negotiation develops from attractive alternatives— the greater your ability to walk away, the stronger your bargaining position.

2. **Minimize perceptual differences:** The way you see something can be quite different from how the other party sees it. Don't assume you know the other person's view: ask questions to gain understanding, and restate your understanding so it can be confirmed or corrected by the other party.

3. **Listen:** Active, attentive listening is mandatory to effective negotiation. Let the other side have an equal share of the air time. (If you're talking more than 50% of the time, you are not listening enough.) In the process, respect silence. Occasionally people need to collect their thoughts before moving ahead. Don't try to fill this time with talking.

4. **Take notes:** You need to know where you are—what has been agreed to; what remains to be resolved. Don't rely on memory. Take notes and then summarize your agreement in a memorandum.

5. **Be creative:** Early closure and criticism stifle creative thinking. Be willing to set some time aside to explore different and unusual ways to solve your problem. During this time, do not permit criticism of ideas offered. All negotiations can benefit from nonjudgmental creative thinking.

Ten Guidelines for Effective Negotiation

6. **Help the other party:** Good negotiators recognize that the other party's problem is their problem as well. Put yourself in the other's position and work to find a solution that meets everyone's needs. After all, no agreement will hold up unless both parties support it.

7. **Make trade-offs:** Avoid giving something for nothing. At least get some goodwill or an obligation for future payback. The basic principle to follow is to trade what is cheap to you but valuable to the other party for what is valuable to you but cheap to the other party.

8. **Be quick to apologize:** An apology is the quickest, surest way to de-escalate negative feelings. It need not be a personal apology. An apology for the situation you're in can be just as effective. Also, don't contribute to hostility by making hostile remarks. Hostility takes the discussion away from the issues and shifts it to a defense of self where the goal is to destroy the opponent.

9. **Avoid ultimatums:** An ultimatum requires the other party to either surrender or fight it out. Neither outcome will contribute to future cooperation. Also, avoid boxing someone in. This happens when you offer only two alternatives, neither of which is desirable to the other person.

10. **Set realistic deadlines:** Many negotiations continue too long because no deadline exists. A deadline requires both sides to be economical in their use of time. It permits you to question the value of certain discussion and encourages both sides to consider concessions and trade-offs in order to meet deadline.

RESOLVING DIFFERENCES

What is best for one department or group won't necessarily be best for others. Out of these differences can come creative solutions when the situation is handled properly. Skill in resolving differences is an important quality of successful project managers.

Consider the model on the following page. Differences can be resolved either *my way, your way,* or *our way.* As a result, four strategies emerge.

Strategies for Resolving Differences
- Demanding
- Problem solving
- Bargaining
- Giving in

(NOT RECOMMENDED)

Model for Resolving Differences

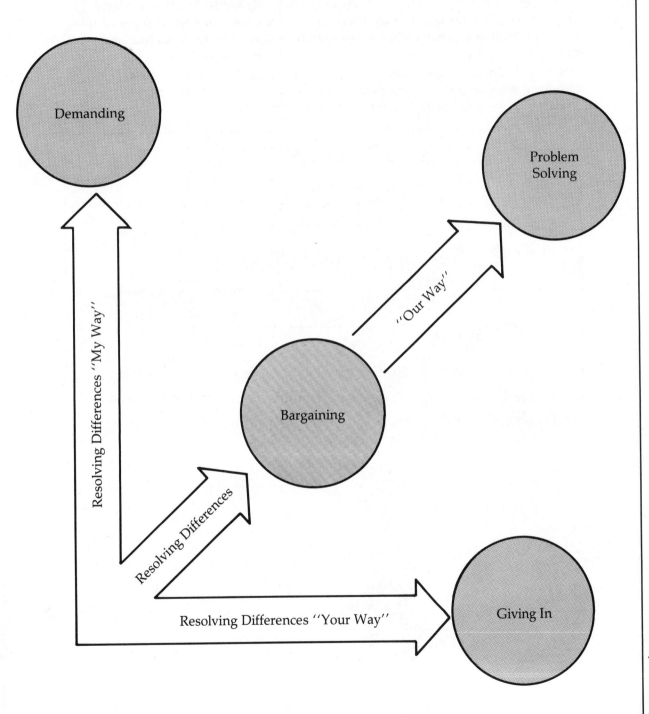

RESOLVING DIFFERENCES (Continued)

The strategy one chooses to resolve differences tends to result from an interplay of assertiveness and cooperation. This process can be clouded by emotion at times, and when this happens, it is difficult to achieve a satisfactory outcome. Therefore, when you sense that either you or the other person's thinking is clouded by emotion, ask to delay discussion a while. The following issues influence assertiveness and cooperation:

Assertiveness

- People tend to be more assertive when an issue is important to them.
- People tend to be more assertive when they are confident of their knowledge.
- People tend to be more assertive when things are going against them.
- People tend to be less assertive when they feel they are at a power disadvantage.

Cooperation

- People tend to be more cooperative when they respect the other person.
- People tend to be more cooperative when they value the relationship.
- People tend to be more cooperative when they are dependent on the other person to help carry out the decision.

RESOLVING DIFFERENCES (Continued)

Given the interplay of assertiveness and cooperation, the following strategies are common for resolving differences:

Demanding: Demanding is high in assertiveness and low in cooperation. It suggests confidence and that the issue is important, coupled with a lack of concern for the relationship and no dependency on the other person.

Problem solving: Problem solving is high in assertiveness, coupled with high cooperation. It suggests that the issue is important, and that there is the need for an ongoing relationship with the other person.

Bargaining: Bargaining is moderate in both assertiveness and cooperation. It suggests that an important issue is being addressed by equally powerful parties. Each must be willing to give a little to reach agreement. Bargaining is also an appropriate backup strategy when joint problem solving seems unattainable.

Giving in: Giving in is low in assertiveness and high in cooperation. The issue may be unimportant to you, you may lack knowledge, or you simply want to go along with the other person's proposal in order to build up the relationship between you.

Each strategy has its place. However, too few people recognize the conditions that support each strategy. Many people adopt one approach for resolving differences and use it in all situations. Obviously, it will be ineffective in many cases. Learn to distinguish among the various types of situations and adopt an approach that has the greatest chance of success in the long run. Don't overlook the importance of maintaining cooperative relationships.

PROGRESS REVIEW: PART 4

Check either *True* or *False* in response to each of the following statements.

True   False

☐   ☐   1. Negotiating for materials, supplies, and services is not a part of a project manager's duties.

☐   ☐   2. Controlling is the central activity during the implementation phase of a project.

☐   ☐   3. Specifications, schedules, and budgets developed during the planning phase become the standards against which actual progress is measured in the implementation phase.

☐   ☐   4. Control point identification usually does not save time.

☐   ☐   5. A project control chart summarizes information on the quality dimension of a project.

☐   ☐   6. A milestone chart is less detailed than required for project planning.

☐   ☐   7. Budget data does not adapt to line graph presentation for monitoring progress.

☐   ☐   8. Testing provides important information on the quality dimension of a project.

☐   ☐   9. Personal inspection is the least effective way to monitor project progress.

☐   ☐   10. Audits are done only at the end of projects to see whether the project is over budget.

☐   ☐   11. An interim progress review requires good listening skills.

☐   ☐   12. All off-specification work should be redone.

☐   ☐   13. Lost time can often be made up on later steps of the project.

True   False

☐   ☐   14. Deploying more resources may save money for the client in the long run.

☐   ☐   15. It is never acceptable to renegotiate the terms of the project after it is under way.

☐   ☐   16. Effective feedback focuses on actions, results, and reaction to them.

☐   ☐   17. It is not important to communicate clearly when giving feedback, because the other person already knows what you are talking about.

☐   ☐   18. Successful negotiating requires a power advantage over the other person.

☐   ☐   19. You have power in negotiation when you have attractive alternatives.

☐   ☐   20. Giving in is never an acceptable strategy for resolving differences.

Score Your Responses

1.—F	4.—F	7.—F	10.—F	13.—T	16.—T	19.—T
2.—T	5.—F	8.—T	11.—T	14.—T	17.—F	20.—F
3.—T	6.—T	9.—F	12.—F	15.—F	18.—F	

Total Score: _____

12 to 15   *Excellent.* You're right on track. Proceed to the next section and keep up the good work.

9 to 11   *Good.* You missed some important information. Review this section before proceeding.

0 to 8   *Poor.* Did you doze off? Reread the section and redo this review before proceeding.

PART 5

COMPLETING
THE PROJECT

BRINGING THE PROJECT TO A SUCCESSFUL CONCLUSION

The goal of project management is to obtain client acceptance of the project result. This means that the client agrees that the quality specifications of the project parameters have been met. In order to have this go smoothly, the client and project manager must have well-documented criteria of performance in place from the beginning of the project. This is not to say that nothing can change, but when changes are made, the contract must be amended to list the changes in specifications along with any resulting changes in schedule and budget.

Objective, measurable criteria are always best, while subjective criteria are risky and subject to interpretation. There should be no room for doubt or ambiguity, although this is often difficult to achieve. It is also important to be clear about what the project output is expected to accomplish. For instance, these three outcomes may produce entirely different results; the project product performs the specified functions; it was built according to approved design; or it solves the client's problem.

The project may or may not be complete when results are delivered to the client. Often there are documentation requirements such as operation manuals, complete drawings, and a final report which usually follow delivery. There may also be people to be trained to operate the new facility or product, and a final audit is common.

Finally, project team members need to be reassigned; surplus equipment, materials, and supplies disposed of; and facilities released.

The final step of any project should be an evaluation review. This is a look back over the project to see what was learned that will contribute to the success of future projects. This review is best done by the core project team and typically in a group discussion.

PROJECT COMPLETION CHECKLIST FOLLOWS

Project Completion Checklist

☐   1. Test project output to see that it works.

☐   2. Write operations manual.

☐   3. Complete final drawings.

☐   4. Deliver project output to client.

☐   5. Train client's personnel to operate project output.

☐   6. Reassign project personnel.

☐   7. Dispose of surplus equipment, materials, and supplies.

☐   8. Release facilities.

☐   9. Summarize major problems encountered and their solution.

☐ 10. Document technological advances made.

☐ 11. Summarize recommendations for future research and development.

☐ 12. Summarize lessons learned in dealing with interfaces.

☐ 13. Write performance evaluation reports on all project staff.

☐ 14. Provide feedback on performance to all project staff.

☐ 15. Complete final audit.

☐ 16. Write final report.

☐ 17. Conduct project review with upper management.

☐ 18. Declare the project complete.

Project Evaluation Form

1. How close to scheduled completion was the project actually completed? _____

   _____

2. What did we learn about scheduling that will help us on our next project? ___

   _____

   _____

   _____

3. How close to budget was final project cost? _____

4. What did we learn about budgeting that will help us on our next project? ___

   _____

   _____

   _____

5. Upon completion, did the project output meet client specifications without
   additional work? _____

6. If additional work was required, please describe: _____

   _____

   _____

   _____

7. What did we learn about writing specifications that will help us on our next
   project? _____

   _____

   _____

8. What did we learn about staffing that will help us on our next project? _____

   _____

   _____

9. What did we learn about monitoring performance that will help us on our next project? _____

_____

_____

_____

10. What did we learn about taking corrective action that will help us on our next project? _____

_____

_____

_____

11. What technological advances were made on this project? _____

12. What tools and techniques were developed that will be useful on our next project? _____

_____

_____

_____

13. What recommendations do we have for future research and development? ___

_____

_____

_____

14. What lessons did we learn from our dealings with service organizations and outside vendors? _____

_____

_____

_____

15. If we had the opportunity to do the project over, what would we do differently? _____

_____

_____

_____

PROGRESS REVIEW: PART 5

Check either *True* or *False* in response to each of the following statements.

True   False

- [ ] [ ]   1. The work of a project manager ends with the delivery of the project output to the client.

- [ ] [ ]   2. The criteria of performance must be agreed to by the client before the project gets under way.

- [ ] [ ]   3. Objective, measurable criteria of performance are easy to develop.

- [ ] [ ]   4. Writing operations manuals and training client personnel in the operation of project output are part of the completion phase.

- [ ] [ ]   5. There is usually no surplus equipment, materials, or supplies to worry about at the end of a project.

- [ ] [ ]   6. The reassignment of project team personnel is one of the final steps in closing down a project.

- [ ] [ ]   7. Typically, the completion of a final audit and the writing of a final report concludes the project manager's responsibilities.

- [ ] [ ]   8. After a project is completed, little can be gained from spending time evaluating the experience.

- [ ] [ ]   9. Projects often make technological advances that are worth sharing with other parts of the organization.

- [ ] [ ]   10. If they are not recorded, lessons learned during the course of a project are typically lost and must be relearned by future project managers.

Score Your Responses

1.—F	3.—F	5.—F	7.—T	9.—T
2.—T	4.—F	6.—T	8.—F	10.—T

Total Score: _____

9 to 10   *Excellent.* You're ready to take on a project and put the knowledge you have gained to productive use.

6 to 8   *Good.* You need some more study of the final phase of a project. A quick review should do it.

0 to 5   *Poor.* You didn't get much from reading this section. I suggest you do it again with more attention to the message.

PART 6

SUMMARY

A MODEL FOR SUCCESSFUL PROJECT MANAGEMENT

Projects are temporary undertakings that have a definite beginning and end. This quality distinguishes them from the ongoing work of an organization. There are four phases in any successful project: defining, planning, implementing, and completing. The diagram shown on page 84 summarizes these phases.

It is imperative to the success of a project that it be clearly defined before it is undertaken. Any definition should include the criteria for determining successful completion of the project. It is reasonable to expect changes to occur once the project is under way, but these changes should be documented along with any resulting impact on schedule and budget.

A succesful project produces an outcome that performs as expected, by deadline, and within cost limits. Thus, the three parameters by which a project is planned and controlled are established. Quality is defined by specifications, time is defined by schedule, and costs are defined by a budget.

To carry out the work of the project, a temporary team is usually assembled. This necessitates developing an organization, assigning duties and responsibilities, and training people in their duties. Frequently, policies and procedures are required to clarify how the team is to function during the project.

When work on the project begins, the project manager has many responsibilities. The work of different individuals and groups must be coordinated so that things run smoothly, and the progress of the project must be monitored and measured against plans. When deviations occur, corrective action must be taken. Also, project managers are expected to provide feedback to team members; negotiate for materials, supplies, and services; and help resolve differences that occur.

The goal of the project is to deliver an outcome to the client. When that day finally arrives, there are still things to be done before the project is complete. This includes writing operations manuals; training client personnel on the use of the project output; reassigning project personnel; disposing of surplus equipment materials, and supplies; evaluating the experience; completing a final audit; writing a project report; and conducting a project review with upper management.

Not every project requires the same attention to each of these activities. It will depend upon the type of project you are undertaking, its size and scope, and the type of organization your are affiliated with. Use your own judgment in selecting the steps important to the success of your project.

Best of luck in the projects you undertake. Success can be yours if you use the concepts presented here.

Four Phases of Project Management

PHASE I -
DEFINING

- Determine objectives
- Select strategy

PHASE II -
PLANNING

- Write specifications
- Develop schedule
- Develop budget

PHASE III -
IMPLEMENTING

- Monitor performance
- Take corrective action

PHASE IV -
COMPLETING

- Deliver output
- Wrap up administrative details
- Evaluate the experience

Project Manager's Checklist

☐   1. Define the project.

☐   2. Select a strategy.

☐   3. Develop specifications.

☐   4. Develop a schedule.

☐   5. Develop a budget.

☐   6. Organize the project team.

☐   7. Assign duties and responsibilities.

☐   8. Train new team members.

☐   9. Monitor progress.

☐ 10. Take corrective action.

☐ 11. Provide feedback.

☐ 12. Test final outcome.

☐ 13. Deliver outcome to client.

☐ 14. Write operations manual.

☐ 15. Train client personnel.

☐ 16. Reassign project staff.

☐ 17. Dispose of surplus equipment, materials, and supplies.

☐ 18. Release facilities.

☐ 19. Evaluate project performance.

☐ 20. Complete final audit.

☐ 21. Complete project report.

☐ 22. Review project with management.

ABOUT THE FIFTY-MINUTE SERIES

We hope you enjoyed this book and found it valuable. If so, we have good news for you. This title is part of the best selling *FIFTY-MINUTE Series* of books. All *Series* books are similar in size and format, and identical in price. Several are supported with training videos. These are identified by the symbol **ⓥ** next to the title.

Since the first *FIFTY-MINUTE* book appeared in 1986, millions of copies have been sold worldwide. Each book was developed with the reader in mind. The result is a concise, high quality module written in a positive, readable self-study format.

FIFTY-MINUTE Books and Videos are available from your distributor. A free current catalog is available on request from Crisp Publications, Inc., 95 First Street, Los Altos, CA 94022.

Following is a complete list of *FIFTY-MINUTE Series* Books and Videos organized by general subject area.

Management Training:

Human Resources & Wellness (continued):

Communications & Creativity:

Customer Service/Sales Training:

Small Business & Financial Planning:

Adult Literacy & Learning:

Career/Retirement & Life Planning: